INSIDE OUT

REBUILDING SELF

AND PERSONALITY

THROUGH

INNER CHILD THERAPY

THERAPIST MANUAL

Ann E. Potter, Ph.D.

Accelerated Development Inc.
Publishers
Muncie, Indiana

Inside Out
Rebuilding Self and Personality through Inner Child Therapy
Therapist Manual

Technical Development: Cynthia Long
Marguerite Mader
Sheila Sheward

ISBN: 1-55959-063-7

Order additional copies from

ACCELERATED DEVELOPMENT INC., Publishers
3808 West Kilgore Avenue
Muncie, Indiana 47304-4896
Toll Free Order Number 1-800-222-1166

DEDICATION

to the helping professionals

who have courage enough

to do their own work.

ACKNOWLEDGEMENTS

I would like to thank my family without whom I would not be who I am and where I am today. My thanks and my love to my family of choice for all their unfailing love, support, and belief in me.

Thanks to Blessed Sacrament Grade School, Marian High School, Creighton University, and the Universities of Nebraska at Omaha and Lincoln for my education.

Thanks to my friends and colleagues for their support and for reviewing the manuscripts and making suggestions, to Dr. Joseph Hollis for his editing expertise, to Roberta Hagemann for her cheerful and patient typing and retyping of the manuscripts, to Pat Bennett for photographing me, and to Shay Neal and Dawn for their help with the graphic designs.

My appreciation and respect to my therapist, my sponsors, and the people of 12-step programs who safely guided my own recovery.

No words can adequately describe my gratitude to my clients and former clients with whom I have had the privilege to do therapy and my colleagues whom I have had the pleasure to train and supervise. I learned more than you'll ever know.

Lastly, I am indebted to my own Higher Power who has led me through pain to joy, grief to release, shyness and insecurity to self-confidence, anger to acceptance and forgiveness, and a lack of direction to a sense of purpose and meaning.

TABLE OF CONTENTS

LIST OF DIAGRAMS

INTRODUCTION

This book is partly my story as an individual and as a professional. Inner Child Therapy is the integration of a personal journey and a professional process. I was familiar with Inner Child work through my own personal experience of healing childhood memories, through my professional training, and through doing Inner Child work with clients. As a result, I developed ideas about strengthening and completing Inner Child work into a whole therapeutic process that goes beyond healing childhood trauma. The sequence of Inner Child work was expanded to include (a) healing of the self and personality; (b) letting go of unhealthy ties to real-life abusers; (c) learning to self-parent; (d) facing and embracing of what Carl Jung called people's "dark side"; (e) encouraging the adult part of people to begin to make healthy decisions, to be "grownups"; and (f) incorporating a solid theoretical base from the counseling and psychology fields throughout the process. Thus, Inner Child Therapy was born.

The alcoholism field and in particular, the Adult Children of Alcoholics movement, offered leadership for the helping profession to explore childhood trauma in a new way. Inner Child work became popular in the last decade or so and involves the healing of painful childhood memories at a deep, psychological level; many times utilizing the reexperience of traumatic events from childhood through hypnosis, guided imagery, or other methods to facilitate healing and growth.

Both personally and professionally, I have found recovering childhood memories to be a particularly challenging part of therapy since the inner child(ren) need protection and special nurturing. They do not automatically know how to function in the adult world. They do not instinctively know how to set good interpersonal boundaries and use problem-solving skills. I remember wandering around at the Veterans Administration Medical Center (VAMC) in Houston, Texas, after reexperiencing a traumatic memory the previous day, feeling like a very scared and vulnerable four year old and being expected to do therapy and behave like an adult. Not until months later, after making some very tragic decisions, did I begin the slow process of healing the other parts of myself and my personality that also had been wounded and whose growth also had been stunted.

Inner Child Therapy has its roots in the therapy in which I participated as an incest survivor. My therapist later became my mentor for a brief time and taught me the groundwork for what I now call Inner Child Therapy. I also gained from Survivors' Week at the Meadows in Arizona and from Pia Melody's and John Bradshaw's work. *I then anchored my experiential knowledge in the foundation of the transtheoretical approach to counseling: especially Transactional Analysis, and Gestalt, cognitive, and behavioral therapies from my training as a counseling psychologist.*

Emotional and psychological safety is a key issue in Inner Child Therapy. Throughout the sequence, people are taught ways to protect themselves as much as possible from the pain caused by feelings of shame and self-hatred often triggered by telling the truth about childhood abuse.

Inner Child Therapy is an imperfect process. However, just as I do at the beginning of a workshop, I disclaim being the "Higher Power" of the results of Inner Child Therapy and claim my belief that the work is protected and nurtured by a power greater than all of us by whom the process is safely guided. I also state that I do not ask people to blame their abusers but, rather, hold their abusers accountable for their behavior no matter what their abusers' intentions or wishes.

The main purposes of this book are to (a) share Inner Child Therapy with professionals as a way of healing the Self and personality, (b) teach theoretical foundations of Inner Child Therapy, and (c) offer techniques useful in doing Inner Child Therapy. As a professional who works with adult children, I encourage you as a professional to do your own work first. Parts of this work can be very frightening if you have not embraced your own dark side and if you, as a therapist, have your own damaged boundaries.

Please take care of yourselves. Surround yourselves with people who love and support you. Have fun. Have lives that include doing therapy rather than doing therapy as the center of your lives. Include colleagues and mentors upon whom you can rely for venting feelings, direction, and even supervision.

A client workbook and an audiocassette tape are available for clients that demonstrate exercises and guided imagery sessions. Please note, the audiocassette only includes guided imagery. The workbook contains both guided imagery and exercises. The therapist manual is meant to be used as a part of training and supervision by an Inner Child therapist.

PART I
OVERVIEW OF INNER CHILD THERAPY

Chapter 1

THE PROCESS

Long lasting change calls for different types of therapy during different phases of therapy (Prochaska & DiClemente, 1986; Prochaska, DiClemente, & Norcross, 1992). The transtheoretical approach to therapy addresses the complex, interactive nature of doing therapy that reflects the various dimensions of client, therapist, problems, interventions, and the helping relationship itself. ***Transtheoretical therapy*** views client change as a gradual movement through specific stages rather than a black/white or all/nothing phenomenon. The five stages of change are (a) ***precontemplation***, (b) ***contemplation***, (c) ***preparation***, (d) ***action***, and (e) ***maintenance***.

Therapeutic interventions from different theories, e.g., gestalt, psychodynamic, cognitive, behavioral, etc., are more effective in certain stages of therapy. When choices about interventions are based on client needs within stages of change, client healing is facilitated (Diagram 1.1). The stages of change are utilized in systemizing therapists' selections of specific therapies in the sequence that optimizes their effectiveness.

COUNSELING THEORIES AND STAGES OF CHANGE

The transtheoretical model addresses those factors, influences, or characteristics that are changeable in the therapy setting. Certainly, factors such as neurochemical imbalances, genetics, and psychiatric disorders need adequate attention and clients may need referrals for psychotropic medication.

Stages				
Precontemplation	Contemplation	Preparation*	Action	Maintenance

Behavior Therapy

Adlerian Therapy   Rational-Emotive Therapy
          Cognitive Therapy

Sullivanian Therapy   Couples Communication
          Transactional Analysis

Strategic Therapy   Bowenian Therapy   Structural Therapy

Psychoanalytic Therapies   Gestalt Therapy
          Existential Therapy

←——————————— Client-Centered Therapy ——————————→

Taken from: Prochaska & DiClemente (1986) The Transtheoretical Approach. Handbook of Eclectic Psychotherapy, John C. Norcross (Ed.) New York. Brunner/Mazel, p. 170. *Preparation stage added in 1992.

DIAGRAM 1.1. Counseling theories and stages of change.

Clients in the ***precontemplation stage*** do not realize they have a problem. Their ability to process information is diminished. They do not do much self-evaluation. They have inadequate emotional reactions to the negative aspects of the problem. They are not very open to significant other's concerns. They do very little to move toward change.

Usually a situational or developmental crisis precipitates movement into the next stage of change. The therapist's role in this stage of the client's change is to develop trust and the foundation of a therapeutic relationship. *Adlerian, Strategic, Client-centered*, and *Psychoanalytic Therapies* are most effective in the pre-contemplation stage. In my practice, clients may come with present-day issues about their relationships and not have an awareness of how the roots of these challenges lie in their childhood experiences. I focus my energy on addressing the problems according to the clients' perceptions, developing the therapeutic relationship, gently introducing links between the present and the past, and wait for the inevitable crisis (e.g., divorce demand by a spouse, job loss, etc.) that readies clients for awareness and change.

Clients in the **contemplation stage** are in the initial level of awareness. They are ready to learn about their problems and can be given information in lectures, in reading assignments, and through therapist's observations, confrontations, and interpretations. *Rational-Emotive* and *Cognitive Therapies* and *Transactional Analysis* are useful in the contemplation stage. I give clients books to read. I spend time in sessions or workshops teaching them about shame, personality development, abuse and neglect, and the long-term effects of abuse and neglect.

Preparation is a stage that bridges between the contemplation and action stages. Clients in the preparation stage are intending to make actual behavioral changes in the near future. Usually, they have failed to make changes in the recent past. They make the shift between awareness and action through small changes in problem behaviors before they modify behaviors completely. Therapies effective in the contemplation and action stages assist clients in moving toward taking action.

I ask clients to weigh the advantages and disadvantages of changing, to evaluate their support system, and to explore their fears and the impact of change on their lives. I encourage clients to investigate options for change through phone calls, attendance at support group meetings, or talking with friends and acquaintances. I help clients brainstorm ideas for intermediate steps towards their ultimate behavioral change goals. For example, someone who is a compulsive overeater may call to find out Overeaters' Anonymous (OA) meeting times, attend an OA meeting, or begin to alter their eating behavior in a small way.

Clients in the **action phase** are ready to actualize their new cognitive learning, to make their changes real. They are taught skills or how to apply skills. *Relapse prevention* is an important aspect of the action phase. I use interventions that bring clients into the "here-and-now" with their feelings in order to deepen the level at which their personal transformation takes place. *Gestalt Therapy* is often helpful in the action phase.

Clients in the **maintenance stage** make their changes lasting and successful in a variety of conditions. *Problem-solving* is an invaluable tool for attaining long-term changes. *Behavior Therapy* is advantageous in the action and maintenance stages. Clients who are preparing to leave therapy with me taper out of therapy over a four month period. They use the last four months to discuss situations in which they are trying new behaviors, new boundaries, etc. and to learn how to identify and analyze their patterns.

Clients may complete only one stage before leaving therapy. Timing in therapy is a key factor. Clients may do their work a stage at a time and their termination of therapy can be positively reframed in light of the stage they completed. The door then can be left open for a client's return when it's time for him/her to do the next stage of healing.

APPROACHES AND THERAPIES UTILIZED

Thus, *Inner Child (I.C.) Therapy is based on the transtheoretical approach to therapy.* I.C. Therapy expands and strengthens the more experiential Inner Child work of John Bradshaw and other adult children of alcoholics therapists and gives I.C. work a sound theoretical foundation.

The **underlying assumptions** of Inner Child (I.C.) Therapy are (a) the past is important when it affects people's ability to function in the present-day; (b) people are capable of working

Stages				
Precontemplation	**Contemplation**	**Preparation**	**Action**	**Maintenance**

Client-Centered Therapy   ——————————————————————————→

         Cognitive Therapy
           - bibliotherapy
           - lectures & discussion

                         Transactional Analysis
                           Gestalt Therapy

                                     Behavior Therapy

DIAGRAM 1.2. Inner Child Therapy in transtheoretical model.

through childhood issues, understanding past decisions, and making new choices; and (c) healing at a deep level occurs when people go beyond talking to make contact with their experience and feelings (Corey, 1982). *Transactional Analysis* is employed throughout the process of I.C. Therapy as the distorted and wounded personality parts are healed and transformed into healthy, cooperative components meant to offer people energy, direction, and structure. *Gestalt Therapy* is utilized to bring feelings about the past into the present for healing and to learn to be one's own inner parents through guided imagery, visualization, parts' work, and empty chair work. *Cognitive Therapy* assists people in forgiveness and in making new choices based on an accurate view of reality and a healthy self-respect. *Behavior Therapy* helps clients translate their new ways of thinking and feeling into healthier actions. (See Diagram 1.2.)

Diagram 1.3 is an **Inner Child Therapy Checklist** that therapists may utilize as an outline for the therapy process, moving clients through the transtheoretical stages of change. The checklist also offers an easy guide to steps of Inner Child Therapy, delineating the reading assignments, visualizations, and exercises for each step.

INNER CHILD THERAPY CHECKLIST

I. PREPARATION (Contemplation and Preparation Stages)

____Information re: shame, codependency, addictions, etc. (Workbook Chapters 1 & 2)

____Exercise 2.1: Spiritual Essence

____Exercise 2.2: Toxic Shame

____Exercise 2.3: Toxic Shame Drawing

____Information re: Childhood and Personality Development (Workbook Chapters 3 & 4)

____Exercise 3.1: Development

____Exercise 4.1: Personality Parts

____Exercise 4.2: Personality Parts' Dialogue

____Information re: Abuse and Neglect (Workbook Chapter 5)

____Exercise 5.1: Examples of Abuse and Neglect

____Information re: Long-term Effects of Abuse and Neglect (Workbook Chapter 5)

____Exercise 5.2: Effects of Abuse and Neglect

____Visualization #1: A Safe Place and Higher Power for the Child (Workbook Chapter 6)

____Exercise 6.1: Inner Child, Safe Place, and Higher Power

____Visualization #3: Initial Negotiations with the Protector-Controller and Offender

____Parts' Work

____

II. TELLING THE TRUTH (Action stage)

____Visualization #2: Embracing the Child (Workbook Chapter 6)

____Parts' work

____Exercise 6.2: List Work

____Exercise 6.3: Adult-Child Letters About Abuse and Neglect

____Exercise 6.4: Higher Power

____

III. FEELINGS WORK (Action Stage)

____Exercise 6.5: Body Locations for Feelings

____Information about family of origin, birth order, genograms, carried feelings, etc. (Workbook Chapter 7.)

____Exercise 7.1: Genogram

___Visualization #6: Healing Traumatic Childhood Memories
___Visualization #4: Carried Feelings
___Exercise 7.2: Carried Feelings
___Visualization #5: Returning Carried Feelings
___Exercise 7.3: Feelings About Abuse and Neglect
___Expressive Therapies

____

IV.RECOGNIZING THE PATTERNS (Action and Maintenance Phases)

___Information re: Parenting, Children's Needs, etc. (Workbook Chapter 10)
___Exercise 10.1: New Parent-Child Letters
___Information re: Boundaries (Workbook Chapter 10)
___Visualization #8: Boundaries
___Exercise 10.2: Boundaries
___Information re: Offender (Workbook Chapter 9)
___Exercise 9.1: Offender Messages
___Visualization #7: Changing the Mind Room
___Information re: Adult needs and functions, problem-solving, forgiveness, affirmations, etc. (Workbook Chapter 11)
___Exercise 11.1: Affirmations
___Exercise 11.2: Letter(s) to Real-Life Offender(s)
___Parts' work

____

V.REINTEGRATION (Maintenance)

___Exercise 11.3: Adult-Offender Letters (Workbook Chapter 11)
___Exercise 11.4: Adult-Protector-Controller Letters
___Exercise 11.5: Adult-Child Letters
___Parts' work
___Visualization #9: Reintegration

____

DIAGRAM 1.3. Inner Child Therapy checklist

(May be photocopied for use by therapist.)

MAJOR STEPS

Inner Child Therapy contains *five main steps*:

1. Cognitive preparation and separation of the personality parts of the Wounded Child, the Offender, and the Protector-Controller (contemplation and preparation stages).

2. Telling the truth about childhood abuse and neglect (action stage).

3. Embracing and feeling the feelings (action stage).

4. Identifying the inner dialogue among the personality parts and ways in which present-day acting-out behavior is related to the dialogue (action and maintenance stages).

5. Bringing about reintegration of the personality parts by healing the Child, reparenting the Child, empowering the Adult, and applying the I.C. process to adulthood issues (maintenance stage).

In the first step, the safety of the **Wounded Child** is insured by giving it a safe place and a Higher Power for protection and nurturance. Essential to the process, the Child is then safe from the **Offender messages** which in the past had set off a self-destructive chain reaction. The **Protector-Controller** is consulted to grant permission for the feeling work to follow and to negotiate the pace of the healing. Cognitive information is given to provide a foundation for the feelings work to follow.

In the second step, the Child then is able to tell the truth about the abuse and neglect from a position of safety.

In the third step, the Adult, not the Child, embraces and works through those feelings. The Child has gone through the experiences once before and so a vital condition for constructive change is for the Child to remain in its safe place with its Higher Power, free to be a child, while the Adult acts as the Child's advocate and does the present-day feelings work. People are educated in detail about types of abuse and the long-term effects of abuse and then they list occurrences of abuse and neglect in their childhoods.   They write letters to and from their inner child(ren) to restart a healthy communication pattern and reestablish the leadership of the Adult (with the help of a Higher Power).

In the fourth step, people recognize their unique pattern of inner dialogue among the personality parts and how that dialogue is related to adulthood behaviors and patterns of interaction. Once identified, the behaviors lose their significance and their power.

The fifth step includes reintegrating the personality parts in a functional way. First, the Offender is separated and real-life offenders (persons who perpetrated the abuse and neglect) are confronted symbolically in therapy. Feelings transferred to the Child during the trauma and carried by the Child are returned to the real-life offenders. Unhealthy parent-child ties are severed and new boundaries are set.   The Offender part is put into perspective and whatever gifts the Offender has that might be useful are identified and taken with the Adult as he/she continues the journey of healing.

Next, the Child's role is clarified and the Nurturing and Protective Parent (formerly the Offender) is taught to set new boundaries.   The functional Parent teaches the Child skills needed for safe and healthy development. Finally, the Adult is empowered by the recognition of and the refuting of Offender messages and converting those messages into affirmations. The Adult then is ready to make new choices about present-day behaviors and about letting go of the past. Forgiveness then can be a decision to let go of unhealthy relationships springing from a solid base of adult self-love and functional boundaries. Adulthood issues can be viewed and resolved through application of skills learned during the I.C. Therapy process.

GUIDELINES FOR THERAPY

Information about the transtheoretical model is helpful in placing clients on a continuum of stages of therapy/change. Through information clients give me during the initial interview,

I assess in what stage of therapy or change they are. Then I can apply appropriate therapy tools from that stage.

Most clients who come to see me for therapy know that I am an expert in Inner Child Therapy so I rarely see people in the precontemplation stage. The majority of clients are in the contemplation stage so I begin therapy with reading assignments and instruction in sessions.

I am often asked the following questions in training:

1. How do you know when a client needs to do Inner Child Therapy?

2. How do you introduce the idea of Inner Child Therapy to clients?

3. How do you initiate Inner Child Therapy with a client who has been working on other issues?

4. How do you decide in what context (4-day treatment program, group or individual therapy) Inner Child Therapy will be done?

5. Are there any kinds of clients with whom you do not do Inner Child Therapy?

Clients Treated

Let me start by saying that I have a philosophical and theoretical bias that adulthood problems have as their roots unresolved childhood issues. So, clients who present complaints such as addictive or compulsive behaviors, chronic anxiety (anxiety/panic attacks), depression, relationship problems, or difficulties parenting their own children usually present dysfunctional experiences in childhood and/or adolescence. I ask questions in the initial interview as a part of a general assessment about clients' family of origin (e.g., "What was your mother/father like as you were growing up?" "How would you describe your parents' marriage?" "How did it feel to grow up in your home?") When I ask about specific types of abuse/neglect, I may give clients general examples of each category. I also ask what clients already know about Inner Child Therapy, what they have read, and what therapy work they have previously done.

So, by the end of the interview, I have an initial understanding of unresolved issues.

I then ask clients what their goals for therapy are. I ask how they might see adulthood problems related to childhood experiences. I do some initial teaching of the links between childhood and adulthood issues. Depending on the clients' response, I would then give clients an initial reading assignment in one of the books mentioned in Chapter Two of the *Manual* or for the first five chapters in the *Workbook*. Every time a client responds to an assignment, I utilize that information as an assessment of the client's stage of therapy/change.

Limitations

I have a few exceptions to this usual process. Of course, I include questions in the initial assessment in order to determine a DSM-III-R or DSM-IV diagnosis. I do not recommend the complete Inner Child Therapy process for clients with an acute thought disorder, antisocial personality disorder, acute bipolar disorder, or multiple personality disorder. I may not do Inner Child Therapy with persons who have a thought disorder in remission. I have found that Inner Child Therapy is helpful in treatment of other personality disorders, even borderline personality disorder; mood disorders; anxiety disorders; post-traumatic stress disorders, and dissociative disorders. Even with clients for whom I decide the complete I.C.T. process is not appropriate, some components such as cognitive information or selected visualizations and exercises may still be helpful.

Group Versus Individual Treatment Modality

Another of my biases is that Inner Child Therapy is best done in a group setting. Group therapy as a treatment modality decreases emotional and social isolation, offers a rich source of feedback, and often begins the development of a healthy support system. Those benefits of group therapy are crucial in the success of Inner Child Therapy. I strongly encourage clients to join related 12-step programs or other community-based support groups. I may see clients for individual therapy instead of group therapy if they refuse to participate in a group or in addition to group therapy if they have severe, chronic issues and/or a serious psychiatric diagnosis.

Treatment Sessions: Number and Length of Time

I see clients for 50-minute individual sessions. Some therapists extend individual sessions to 90 minutes in length. Usually, Inner Child Therapy can be completed in 12 to 14 individual sessions (approximately six to seven months if sessions are held every other week.) I use weekly, 90-minute sessions for group therapy. Some therapists utilize two hour groups. The Inner Child Therapy process can be finished in 21 group sessions (approximately five to six months) or a 4-day outpatient program.

THERAPIST ACTIVITIES

1. Review transtheoretical stages of change/therapy.

2. Review five steps of Inner Child Therapy.

3. Include questions in initial assessment with client about family of origin issues. Assess client in light of stage of therapy/change. Assess client's readiness to do Inner Child Therapy. Clarify your and client's goals.

4. Decide with client what treatment modalities would be appropriate, e.g., intensive treatment, group and/or individual therapy.

5. Initiate checklist for client.

THE SELF AND SHAME

Chapter 2 in the *Workbook* covers the definitions of **self, personality**, and **shame**. Spirituality is an essential concept to Inner Child Therapy and is integrated into the psychology and counseling theories through the idea of a "spiritual essence."

The progression of the development of Self from Spiritual Essence to adulthood behaviors is illustrated in Diagram 2.3 that is included in the *Workbook*. Healthy childhood experiences that lead to healthy shame, a balanced sense of self, and functional adult behaviors are distinguished from abusive and neglectful childhood experiences that lead to toxic shame, codependency, and dysfunctional adult behaviors.

GUIDELINES FOR THERAPY

When adult children come to therapy in the precontemplation stage and do not see their past as an issue, I usually address their presenting complaints and work on developing trust and healthy attachment. This groundwork is critical to the success of future therapeutic interventions when clients begin to recognize how traumatic childhoods impact their adult lives.

Levels of Therapy

Inner Child Therapy is done at least on two different levels: (a) addressing the tangible issues and (b) correcting parenting experiences through the client-therapist relationship. Many adult children suffered ineffective bonding with their parents; they were not able to experience unconditional love combined with protective limits. The therapy relationship is an opportunity for clients to establish a healthy attachment with someone who models caring and firm boundaries. The original bond then is corrected and clients are taught to become individuals who are capable of both autonomy and mutuality.

Shame reduction is a very significant component to early Inner Child therapy. Simple interventions such as asking clients to make eye contact during feedback can help clients feel less isolated and ashamed.

Inner Child Issues of Therapist

For therapists to deal with their own inner child issues is imperative so that their vision of client's issues can be as clear as possible. Therapists who have not settled their own "stuff" typically have "blind spots," have trouble discerning whose problem is whose, and may even project their unresolved issues onto clients. For example, a therapist who has not dealt with incest issues may ignore cues that clients are incest survivors, may minimize client feelings related to incest, may protect the perpetrators and buy into "blaming the victim," or may rush client into decisions about forgiveness.

Therapist as Educator

When adult children enter therapy in the contemplation stage of change, they have a beginning awareness that their past is negatively affecting their adult decisions and choices. An important role for therapists is that of educator. New, accurate information activates the adult part of clients and corrects past misinformation.

I teach clients about shame; how to recognize it, how to discover from where it came, how to decide to whom it belongs, and how to hold abusers responsible for their shameless behavior. I make reading assignments, e.g., *Healing the Shame That Binds Us, Adult Children: Secrets of Dysfunctional Families, The Emotional Incest Syndrome,* or *Healing the Child Within.* I ask people to take notes about what seems to fit for them and write their feelings about what they're reading.

I also may ask them to do "feelings checks" several times a day. They take a list of the six main feelings, e.g., anger, shame, pain, happiness, sadness, and fear, and ask themselves "what am I feeling right now?" I use this exercise particularly with clients who cannot identify or name feelings related to what they're reading for therapy. The basic reading assignments and feeling identification starts to prepare clients for the more intense feeling work ahead.

The purposes of Exercise 2.1, 2.2, and 2.3 in Chapter 2 of the *Workbook* are to assist clients (a) in beginning to identify shame both on a feeling level and through the use of their senses and (b) in beginning to separate shame from themselves and their bodies.

THERAPIST ACTIVITIES

1. Reflect on your own Inner Child issues. If not resolved, find a way to do your own Inner Child process. Not doing so may cause blind spots with clients.

2. Have client study information in Chapter 2 on shame, codependency, addictions, etc. Help client clarify any misunderstandings.

3. Discuss with client *Workbook* material—Diagram 2.1 and Exercise 2.1: Spiritual Essence.

4. Repeat Step 3 with Diagram 2.2 and Exercises 2.2 and 2.3: Toxic Shame.

5. Review Diagram 2.3: Process of Development of Adulthood Behaviors. Help client differentiate the two paths of development.

Chapter **3**

CHILD DEVELOPMENT WHAT'S "NORMAL"

Chapter 3 in the *Workbook* defines normal childhood development and describes the process in four stages. Motor-physical, language, cognitive, emotional, moral, and psychosocial development are outlined in Figure 3.1 in the *Workbook*. Adult children can use this information to clarify for themselves what is "normal" and identify their strengths and weaknesses.

GUIDELINES FOR THERAPY

Childhood development is a very important aspect of Inner Child Therapy. Clients are given needed information about what's "normal" and about their needs and capabilities throughout childhood and adolescence. Clients are able to discern what ages their inner children are by applying new information about development. For example, trust or attachment issues reflect an infant or toddler. Issues with competence tend to suggest a school-age child, whereas rebelliousness would indicate a teenager.

The information contained in Chapter 3 prepares clients for future work with the Inner Child. Clients begin with whatever age emerges in the first visualization (see Chapter 6). They deal with whatever developmental stage surfaces in whatever sequence. For example, a client might begin with a four-year-old child, go on to a toddler-age child, and then to a teenager. The less directive approach allows clients to address their most prevalent issues in the order of their priority.

THERAPIST ACTIVITIES

1. Ask client to study information in Chapter 3 and Figure 3.1.

2. Review Exercise 3.1 with client, stressing how information can be applied to client.

PERSONALITY DEVELOPMENT

The functional personality and how the development process is affected by a dysfunctional family and by childhood experiences of abuse and neglect are explained in Chapter 4 of the *Workbook*. The adapted child personality part becomes the Wounded/Broken-hearted Child, the Protective Parent becomes the Offender, and the Adult becomes the Protector-Controller, (See Diagrams 4.1 and 4.2 in the *Workbook*).

Gestalt parts' work is helpful in distinguishing the personality parts. In so doing, healthy boundaries can be established between the Adult and other personality parts; and each personality part can be eventually reintegrated in a functional way.

GUIDELINES FOR THERAPY

I give clients information directly through lecture or during sessions about childhood and personality development and how both are changed in the context of a dysfunctional family and affected by abuse and neglect. This information is vital to each client's becoming able to distinguish his or her Offender, Protector-Controller, and Child(ren) and detect the messages and behaviors related to each one; the patterns of communication among all the parts; and eventually, how awarenesses are connected to adult life feelings, behaviors, decisions, and problems.

Exercises 4.1 and 4.2 in Chapter 4 of the *Workbook* help clients apply the cognitive information given in lectures or sessions about the self and personality parts. Exercise 4.1 helps clients visually conceptualize the three parts, the strength of each part, and how the three parts relate to each other. Exercise 4.2 promotes client recognition of their inner parts' dialogue and sets in motion the initial separation among parts.

THERAPIST ACTIVITIES

1. Review information with client in Chapter 4 and Diagrams 4.1 and 4.2. Clarify client's understanding of personality parts.

2. Discuss with client results of Exercises 4.1 and 4.2.

PART II
HEALING THE
BROKEN-HEARTED
CHILD

Chapter **5**

EFFECTS OF ABUSE
AND NEGLECT

Chapter 5 in the *Workbook* defines abuse and neglect and differentiates six types of abuse and neglect. Children's responses to childhood trauma are outlined in Diagram 5.1: Chronic Shock. Long-term effects are explored. The concepts of "carried feelings" (see Diagram 5.2) are outlined. The "reality switch" occurring between the real-life offenders and children during the traumatic acts (see Diagram 5.3) are explained.

GUIDELINES FOR THERAPY

Knowledge about abuse and neglect and the long-term effects is critical to recovery and healing. Many adult children use the **defense mechanisms** of denial, rationalization, intellectualization, disassociation, and/or minimization. Their views of their childhoods are fairly distorted. "Other people had it worse," or "It wasn't that bad," or "My parents meant well," or "My parents did the best they could" are common expressions early in therapy. In addition to the use of defense mechanisms, children often are told by their abusers and other adults that their feelings are invalid and that the abuse and neglect aren't that bad.

By this point in therapy clients are well into the contemplation stage of change. They are more connected to their emotions and are able to develop insight from a variety of therapeutic techniques. Gentle confrontation from the therapist in the form of facts and reality testing is a part of breaking through denial and promotes accurate estimates of childhood experiences and the resultant damages. Exercises 5.1 and 5.2 in the client workbook ask clients to make preliminary lists of abusive and/or neglectful childhood experiences and of long-term effects of such experiences.

Sometimes, clients cannot remember much of their childhood. I usually work with what they do remember and do not use hypnosis or other techniques to uncover repressed memories. I do guided imagery with memory fragments and dreams. I have found that needed memories often come back at some point in the process. I tell clients that what they do remember is usually traumatic enough and that we address their actual memories. I use the lists of abuse/neglect examples and let clients name their own traumas. For example, a client came to me for therapy because she had had some contact with her father a few months before she came to me, and she was very angry and depressed about the way he was treating her as an adult. Her history revealed severe emotional, physical, and verbal abuse during childhood. I suspected sexual abuse also, but she had no memories of such abuse. I did not share my suspicions with the client. So, she worked in therapy on the abuse she remembered. After several months of individual therapy, she went through my 3-day, intensive Inner Child workshop, and on the second evening of the workshop, during sex with her husband, she had flashbacks and body memories about sexual abuse by her father.

I do not believe that clients have to remember every traumatic detail in order to heal. I believe that healing the feelings and memories clients do have and completing the unfinished business from those memories and feelings are primarily important.

THERAPIST ACTIVITIES

1. Have client carefully examine information in Chapter 5 on abuse and neglect, long-term effects, and Diagram 5.1, Chronic Shock; Diagram 5.2, Carried Feelings; and Diagram 5.3, Reality Switch.

2. Review Exercise 5.1 and 5.2 to help the client develop an initial understanding of how information in Chapter 5 applies to client's life.

A SAFE PLACE
TO TELL THE TRUTH

Chapter 6 in the *Workbook* details how clients create a position of safety and nurturance from which their inner children may tell the truth about childhood abuse and neglect. The development of a **Safe Place** and **Higher Power** for both the Adult and the Child(ren) minimizes negative reactions to betraying the family secrets (usually from the Offender) and allows clients their feelings.

GUIDELINES FOR THERAPY

Clients who are working on the issues in Chapter 6 have moved from the contemplation, through the preparation, to the action stage of change. Clients often spend some time in therapy "preparing" to take action. After they have awareness and knowledge, they take initial steps towards changing problem behaviors that would be defined better as the preparation rather than action stage. Once in the action stage, processing and healing now are at a deeper level and cognitive information is used as a foundation for intense feeling work and the beginning toward restructuring of Self and the personality.

Visualization #1 (A Safe Place and Higher Power for the Child) and Exercise 6.1 in Chapter 6 of the *Workbook* are means of helping clients to address the important components of a Safe Place and a Higher Power. In Visualization #2 (Embracing the Child), clients are helped to reclaim repressed childhood feelings. In Exercises 6.2 and 6.3, clients are requested to give more detailed information about childhood abuse and neglect and help clients reconnect feelings with specific memories. Clients use their nondominant hand whenever they write from any of their inner children. This technique bypasses the logical, rational left brain and accesses the nonverbal, emotional, intuitive right brain (Capacchione, 1991).

In Visualization #3 (Initial Negotiation with Protector-Controller and Offender), the initial personality parts' division and negotiation of new roles for the Protector-Controller and the Offender are accomplished. Exercise 6.4 helps clients clarify their relationship with a Higher Power.

In Visualization #4 (Carried Feelings) and Exercise 6.5, clients are assisted in naming carried feelings and describing the body locations of the carried feelings.

THERAPIST ACTIVITIES

1. Ask client to read information in Chapter 6.

2. Explore client's readiness to begin action stage. Review steps the client already has taken toward changing. Assess support system. Evaluate advantages and disadvantages of beginning feelings work. If the client does not seem ready to proceed, return to activities from contemplation stage or evaluate appropriateness of terminating this phase of therapy. If the client appears ready to begin feelings work, complete Step 3.

3. Take client through Visualization #1. Review information from Visualization #1 and Exercises 6.1 and 6.4. Make sure Safe Places and Higher Powers are both protective and nurturing.

4. Do Visualization #3 with client. Ask client questions to discern level of Offender's and Protector-Controller's cooperation in becoming more positive.

5. Begin to correct relationships among personality parts through parts' work with client.

6. Examine in depth with client childhood traumatic experiences through Exercises 6.2 and 6.3.

7. Begin feelings work by going over identified feelings and where client feels the feelings in his/her body illustrated in Exercise 6.5. Review Visualization #4.

A CLOSER LOOK
AT FAMILY OF ORIGIN

Through Chapter 7 in the *Workbook*, the client explores family systems theory concepts such as roles and birth order. Clients are taught how to design a family genogram (see Diagram 7.2). Clients begin to sort through feelings, decide what feelings belong to them, and return the other feelings to the people from whom the feelings originated.

GUIDELINES FOR THERAPY

Completion of Exercise 7.1 in the *Workbook* helps clients gain new insights into their family of origin and a structured way to conceptualize patterns and relationships. One of the most powerful aspects of Inner Child Therapy is the clients' opportunity to sort through feelings and finally to be accountable only for their own feelings. During Visualization #5 (Returning Carried Feelings) clients specify what feelings both the Child and Adult parts of themselves carry for members of the family of origin and return the carried feelings to the rightful owners. By doing Exercises 7.2 and 7.3, clients again sort through carried feelings and are assisted to name and own their own feelings while letting go of carried feelings.

Please note that clients may be reluctant to return feelings to previous generations. Remind them that they are not responsible for others and do not have to take care of others' feelings. As alternatives, clients can return feelings to family members' Higher Powers or destroy the feelings in some other manner (put them into orbit, bury them, disintegrate them, etc.).

Feelings Work

Feelings work is an essential component of the healing process. Many times, talking about anger, fear, sadness, rage, hopelessness, and shame is not sufficient to express, release, and heal those feelings. *Expressive therapies* and body work often supplement "talk" therapy by tapping into another level of people's feeling reality and allowing feelings to be expressed in nonverbal and less intellectualized, verbal ways. Art, expression, music, abreaction, and dance therapies provide opportunities to release emotional energy through drawing, pounding, throwing, ripping, screaming, crying, and physical movement. *Massage therapy* and other forms of body work facilitate the release of emotions stored in the body. These alternative therapies also aid people in resolving feelings from traumatic experiences that happened at a preverbal age (before the age when they could talk).

If some type of expression therapy is not included in sessions, acting as a referral source to clients for local expression or massage therapists is vital to the therapy process. The following list offers a few ideas for facilitating feelings work in sessions:

1. empty-chair work with real-life offenders,
2. screaming into a pillow,
3. throwing or hitting a pillow,
4. using foam bats,
5. drawing/painting pictures,
6. using sand tray play (Weinrib, 1983),
7. ripping up phone books, and/or
8. using visualizations.

Preparation for feelings work includes letters to, dialogues with, or visualizations about putting inner children in Safe Places with Higher Powers with the reminder that they only tell the Adult part what the feelings are, and the Adult is then responsible for expressing and healing the feelings.

Diagram 7.1 details an example of the stages of change through which clients progress while participating in one of the expressive therapies, the Sand Tray process (Weinrib, 1983; Hacker & Potter, 1993). The *initial stage* describes clients' pre-trauma state in which feelings, thoughts, senses, and behavior are integrated, and clients experience a sense of psychological balance. Trauma occurs and clients disassociate their feelings, thoughts, senses, and behavior as a way to psychologically survive the trauma (*pre-therapy stages*).

When clients enter therapy, an expressive therapy such as the Sand Tray is introduced at some point to facilitate feelings work (*therapeutic intervention stages*). Clients place small figures and objects in a large box of sand in order to

1. *externalize* — bring outside themselves threatening, unacceptable, or overwhelming feelings, memories, or situations, and
2. *concretize* — make tangible issues, concerns, or feelings that are abstract, intellectualized, or cut off from consciousness.

Once clients place figures and objects into the sand tray, I ask them to tell me about their tray. I use the BASK model (Braun, 1986) to guide clients in talking about behaviors (who did what when), affect (how did they feel), sensations (what they heard, saw, smelled, felt, and tasted), and resultant knowledge (what really happened, how it makes sense to the clients).

After clients talk about their sand trays, I ask them to make the tray the way they would like it to be or to change the objects and figures in the sand to demonstrate how they would change their feelings, memories, or situations (*correction* process). As a result of being able to "make real" and to correct their internal world, clients then reintegrate their feelings, thoughts, senses, and behavior. They experience *empowerment* and *healing* as they *transition* out of or *complete* their feelings work in therapy.

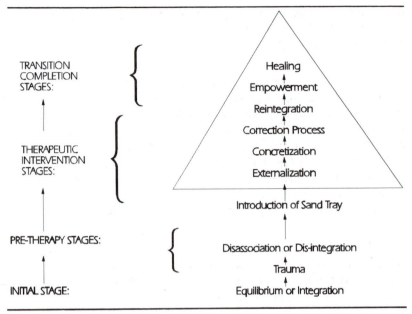

DIAGRAM 7.1. Sand Tray Process. From Hacker & Potter, 1993.
Reprinted with permission.

THERAPIST ACTIVITIES

1. Have client study information in Chapter 7 on family of origin, birth order, genograms, and carried feelings. Discuss information and answer questions.

2. Review client's family of origin genogram from Exercise 7.1.

3. Take client through Visualization #6 to heal a traumatic childhood memory. Discuss how client can use this visualization with other memories or flashbacks.

4. Continue instruction of client about carried feelings through review of Visualization #4 and Exercise 7.2.

5. Assist client in returning carried feelings to real-life offenders through Visualization #5.

6. Review Exercise 7.3 to facilitate client's claiming of own feelings about traumatic experiences.

7. Use expressive therapies with client to assist with feelings work (e.g., anger work, art therapy, etc.) If you aren't comfortable with your training or skills, investigate local resources for referrals.

PART III
PARTS' REINTEGRATION

A CLOSER LOOK AT PERSONALITY PARTS

Through doing Chapter 8 in the *Workbook*, the client is assisted with more extensive work with the personality parts. The Protector-Controller is usually the first part with whom negotiations take place (see Chapter 8 in *Workbook*).

GUIDELINES FOR THERAPY

A key to Inner Child Therapy is respect for and acceptance of the present boundaries set by the Protector-Controller. This part has helped people survive and I am cautious to take away defenses before healthier coping skills have been developed. Sometimes, I will do parts' work with the Protector-Controller to get "permission" to do feeling work with a client.

Cues to Different Parts

Sometimes, another part will come out while I am talking to the Protector-Controller. I pay close attention to changes in tone of voice, facial expression, and body posture. Those nonverbal cues give me hints that another part has "come out." I might then say, "I noticed that you became a little tearful (or . . . your voice changed . . . or . . . you started jiggling your foot) when you said that. How old do you feel right now? (Or . . . Who is talking now?

. . . or . . . Who just came out?) I ask them to move to a different place in the room and become that part to continue the session.

The power of parts' work is in clarifying who the parts are, how they relate to each other, and gaining commitments to negotiate new ways to function.

Goals of Parts' Work

The goals of parts' work are

1. identification of personality parts;

2. separation of enmeshed parts;

3. development of a relationships between each part and therapist;

4. investigation of each part:

   a. the origin/purpose,

   b. the messages,

   c. the ways in which client has been helped/hindered, and

   d. the ways in which adult life is influenced; and

5. negotiation of new behavior from each part and more positive relationships among the parts.

Therapist's Reactions as Cues

A hint to what personality part is being expressed is the therapist's reaction to his/her client at any given time. I find that when the Child is out, I tend to feel sympathetic, protective,and nurturing or angry and suffocated. Some clients have what I call **velcro kids**. These inner kids tend to be very demanding, want to be in charge of the adult's life, and have the attitude that nothing is ever "enough." My cues that a "velcro kid" is involved are the client's intense neediness and subtle dissatisfaction with therapy (e.g., nothing is enough, appearance of expecting more or chronic disappointment).

When someone's Offender is out, I might feel insulted or put down, angry, afraid, or intimidated. I also might feel a need to be right or to argue.　When clients' Protector-Controllers are in charge, I tend to feel distanced, shut out, bored, or frustrated.

THERAPIST ACTIVITIES

1. Do parts' work with client.　Use parts' work to facilitate transformation of personality back to more positive version as illustrated in Diagram 4.1.

2. Develop awareness of your own internal reactions to clients. Use reactions as assessment tool for client's personality parts.

3. Pay close attention to client's nonverbal behavior as clues to personality parts.

DEALING WITH
THE OFFENDER

Through Chapter 9 in the *Workbook*, clients gain a more in-depth examination of the Offender part of the personality. Clients are shown how to confront the Offender and/or real-life offenders through visualizations and letters. Therapy includes parts' work with clients in sessions (see Chapters 8 & 9.)

GUIDELINES FOR THERAPY

During Visualization #6 (Healing Traumatic Childhood Memories) in the client *Workbook*, clients heal traumatic childhood memories by offering themselves ways to rectify the abusive or neglectful occurrences. Some of the corrections in the visualization are (a) rescuing the child from the trauma, (b) putting the child in a Safe Place with a Higher Power, (c) acting as an advocate for the child through reassurances and affirmation, and (d) returning as the adult to confront the real-life offender(s).

Gifts or positive aspects of the childhood trauma may be identified at this point. For example, clients may identify good boundaries, a determination to get better, strength, or empathy as positive points taken from childhood traumas into adulthood. Clients also may write angry letters to or resentment lists about real-life offenders. They also may construct a list of their losses related to childhood trauma and write grief letters along with their angry letters. Anger, sadness, pain, and grief are all covered in the letters.

By completing Exercise 9.1, clients identify Offender messages. Then through Visualization #7 (Changing the Mind Room), clients experientially identify, remove, and replace Offender messages with positive, affirming messages.

THERAPIST ACTIVITIES

1. Discuss with client possible memories for use in Visualization #6. Take client through the visualization, asking him/her to describe sensations, behavior, and thoughts in detail. Encourage expression of feelings. Identify any positive aspects or strengths gained from experiences.

2. Begin process with client of changing the more negative, Offender messages through Exercise 9.1 and Visualization #7. Encourage client to list as many Offender messages as possible.

REPARENTING THE CHILD(REN)

Children's needs (trust, encouragement, boundaries) are outlined in Chapter 10 of the *Workbook*. Clients are supported in learning to parent their own inner children so that the children are not over involved with the adult's life. The Adult part of the personality is freed to make choices based on solid problem-solving skills rather than being based on making attempts to meet unmet childhood needs.

GUIDELINES FOR THERAPY

Exercise 10.1 in the *Workbook* involves letters between the Child part(s) and the New Parent. The Child's needs are addressed as well as the New Parent's capabilities. A new, realistic, nurturing, and protective relationship is negotiated between clients' Child(ren) and the New Parent parts.

Therapists act as healthy parents models for their clients so they learn skills necessary for parenting their inner children. As one of my clients said, "So, Dr. Potter, the way you treat me teaches me how to parent my own (inner) kids."

Through Visualization #8 (Boundaries) and Exercise 10.2, clients are offered the opportunity to develop new boundaries mentally, emotionally, and visually. I recommend that clients practice their new boundaries a couple of times a day (while their brushing teeth even) so that the boundaries become second nature and in threatening situations can be put in place within seconds.

THERAPIST ACTIVITIES

1. Ask client to read information about parenting and children's needs. Brainstorm with client a list of children's needs for nurturance and protection.

2. Review with client New Parent-Child letters from Exercise 10.1. Discuss any distortions (e.g., enmeshment, peer or caretaking role by child, judgement or placating by New Parent) in the new Parent-Child relationships.

3. Reflect on the therapist-client relationship and ways in which you model healthy parenting with your client.

4. Take client through Visualization #8. Generate ideas for flexible, protective boundaries. Encourage client to practice visualizing new boundaries daily. Review Exercise 10.2.

EMPOWERING
THE ADULT

By working through Chapter 11 in the *Workbook*, clients delineate the needs and functions of the Adult part of the personality. Clients are taught how to transform the negative Offender messages into affirmations and problem-solving skills. The process of forgiveness is clarified.

GUIDELINES FOR THERAPY

Clients review Visualization #7 (Changing the Mind Room) and Exercise 9.1 concerning Offender messages because they are going to formalize the transformation from negative messages to affirmations. In Exercise 11.1 in the *Workbook*, the Offender messages are listed again and then replaced with affirmations using the criteria specified in the chapter.

I often use Woititz's and Garner's *Life Skills for Adult Children* book (1990) and *Workbook* (1991) as a resource for clients. Skills such as communication; expressing feelings and needs; listening; problem-solving; fair fighting; and ending relationships offer clients information and options helpful to them in adulthood situations. Hough's *Let's Have It Out* (1991) also teaches healthy confrontation and negotiation skills.

Relationships among Personality Parts

The new, evolving relationships among personality parts (Child or Children, Offender or New Parent, and Protector-Controller or Adult) are defined and refined in the letters from Exercises 11.3, 11.4, and 11.5. The letters serve as official agreements for the healthier ways of thinking, communicating, and behaving among the personality parts. In Exercise 11.2, clients have the opportunity to write letters to real-life offenders in order to return carried feelings and define adulthood relationships with them.

Clients may or may not confront their abusers in their adult life. I recommend people complete their Inner Child Therapy before they make a decision to talk directly with real-life offenders. Clients also need to examine their motives for any confrontation. If they want to express feelings and establish new boundaries, I usually support their decision. If they want a particular response, an admission of guilt or request for forgiveness, or a change in behavior from the other person, I usually suggest they wait until they can make the confrontation for their own growth.

I hope clients eventually come to a balanced viewpoint about their childhoods rather than an all-bad or all-good way of looking at their real-life offenders and their past. Certainly some clients suffered such chronic, severe abuse that nothing positive can be said about real-life offenders. Sometimes, a character strength developed as a result of working through adversity is the positive aspect from the past. Clients list gifts from the past and may write thank-you letters to real-life offenders. Clients write "good-bye" or "letting go" letters when they are ready to put closure on their past relationships with real-life offenders.

I also hope clients come to a balanced self-concept which neither under- nor over-estimates themselves. Helping clients assess their strengths, skills, coping strategies, along with the areas needing improvement leads to a healthy sense of self.

The final visualization (9) symbolizes personality reintegration. The house represents the Self. Initially, clients say good-bye to their old "Self" and take something useful from the old "Self" to the new "Self." Each personality part that is ready to reintegrate has its space while also being a member of the household. This new balance stands for the stability between the individual part with its healthy boundary and the cooperative relationships among the parts as part of the whole personality. Cues about what personality parts need more work are found in the parts that are not ready to yet live in the house.

Maintenance Stage of Change

The Maintenance Stage of change involves transforming new behaviors into behaviors that will last over a long period of time. Inner Child Therapy can be supplemented by couples' therapy or sex therapy to address present-day issues as childhood experiences are resolved and left behind. Shifting back from more affective, here-and-now interventions to cognitive and behavioral strategies accomplishes the transformation. Since Inner Child Therapy is an ongoing process, the tools found in earlier chapters (letter writing, parts' work, affirmations, visualizations, etc.) are applied to continue healing the Self and personality.

THERAPIST ACTIVITIES

1. Ask client to read information about re-empowering the Adult in Chapter 11.

2. Review with client Visualization #7 and Exercise 9.1 to refresh client's memory about Offender messages.

3. Review with client procedure for writing affirmations. Assist client in brainstorming affirmations for Offender messages.

4. Do parts' work with client to continue transformation process of personality parts.

5. Review with clients letters written between Adult and Offender, Child, and Protector-Controller to formalize new roles in Exercises 11.3, 11.4 and 11.5.

6. Discuss with client advantages and disadvantages of directly confronting real-life offenders. Prepare client through

letter-writing and role-playing. Examine client's motives for a confrontation.

7. Reflect on your own attitudes about direct confrontation of real-life offenders and how your attitude may influence your client.

8. Assess level of client's skills in areas such as communication, problem-solving, decision-making, assertiveness, and conflict management. Help client find information, classes, resources to teach needed skills.

9. Encourage the client to examine positive and negative aspects of traumatic experiences.

10. Have client list personal strengths and weaknesses. Assist client to utilize problem-solving process in Chapter 11 in setting goals for making changes.

11. Brainstorm with client how Inner Child Therapy tools can be applied to specific adulthood issues.

12. Take client through Visualization #9. Discuss client's feelings about old and new houses. Determine with client what parts were ready for integration and what parts may need further work.

APPENDIX 1
CLIENT EXERCISES IN WORKBOOK

APPENDIX 2
VISUALIZATIONS IN WORKBOOK

1. A Safe Place and Higher Power for the Child: Chapter 6, p. 57
2. Embracing the Child: Chapter 6, p. 61
3. Initial Negotiation with Protector-Controller and Offender: Chapter 6, p. 61
4. Carried Feelings: Chapter 6, p. 74
5. Returning Carried Feelings: Chapter 7, p. 82
6. Healing Traumatic Childhood Memories: Chapter 9, p. 94
7. Changing the Mind Room, Chapter 9, p. 100
8. Boundaries: Chapter 10, p. 113
9. Reintegration — The House: Chapter 11, p. 140

APPENDIX 3
WORKBOOK FIGURES

3.1 Development through Childhood and Adolescence: Chapter 3, pp. 22-26
7.1 CATHY cartoon: Chapter 7, p. 75
7.2 Laurie Lipton, Facing up to Reality: Chapter 7, p. 85

APPENDIX 4
WORKBOOK DIAGRAMS

2.1 Spiritual essence: Chapter 2, p. 10
2.2 Toxic shame: Chapter 2, p. 13
2.3 Process of development of adult behaviors: Chapter 2, p. 14
4.1 Healthy personality: Chapter 4, p. 34
4.2 Dysfunctional personality: Chapter 4, p. 35
5.1 Chronic shock: Chapter 5, p. 49
5.2 Carried feelings: Chapter 5, p. 51
5.3 Reality switch: Chapter 5, p. 52
6.1 List work: Chapter 6, pp. 63-65
7.2 The McDonald family genogram: Chapter 7, p. 79
10.1 Functional boundaries: Chapter 10, p. 111
10.2 Dysfunctional boundaries: Chapter 10, p. 112

BIBLIOGRAPHY

Achenbach, T.M. (1982). *Developmental psychopathology* (2nd ed.) New York: John Wiley & Sons.

Adams, L. (1979). *Effectiveness training for women.* New York: Wyden Books.

American Psychiatric Association. (1987). *Diagnostic and statistical manual of mental disorders* (3rd-revised). Washington, DC: Author.

Battegay, R. (1991). *The hunger diseases.* Toronto, Canada: Hogrefe & Huber Publishers.

Black, C. (1983). *It will never happen to me.* New York: Ballantine Books.

Blume, E.S. (1990). *Secret survivors.* New York: John Wiley & Sons.

Bowlby, J. (1969). *Attachment.* New York: Basic Books.

Bradshaw, J. (1988). *Healing the shame that binds you.* Deerfield Beach, FL: Health Communications.

Braun, B. (1986). *Treatment of multiple personality disorder: Issues in the psychotherapy of multiple personality disorder.* Washington, DC: American Psychiatric Press.

Capacchione, L. (1991). *Recovery of your inner child.* New York: Simon & Schuster.

Cherry, B. (1987). *Childhood sexual abuse.* Workshop presented at Supportive Services in Houston, Texas.

Cline, F.W. (1982). *Parent education text.* Evergreen, CO: Evergreen Consultants in Human Behavior.

Corey, G. (1982). *Theory and practice of counseling and psychotherapy* (2nd ed). Monterey, CA: Brooks/Cole Publishing.

Covey, S.R. (1989). *The seven habits of highly effective people.* New York: Simon & Schuster.

Emery, H.G., & Brewster, K.G. (Eds.). (1933). *The new century dictionary.* New York: D. Appleton-Century.

Estés, C.P. (1992). *Women who run with wolves.* New York: Ballantine Books.

Greenspan, G.I. (1989). *The development of the ego: Implications for personality theory, psychopathology, and the therapeutic process.* Madison, WI: International Universities Press.

Groves, D. (1986). *Healing the wounded child within.* A set of audiotapes and workbook. Munster, IN: David Grove Seminars.

Hacker, C., & Potter, A. (1993). *Sand tray therapy with dissociative disorders.* Paper presented at International Dissociative Disorders convention; Chicago, Illinois.

Harper, J., & Hoopes, M. (1990). *Uncovering shame.* New York: W.W. Norton.

Hazelton Foundation. (1991). *Talk, trust, feel.* New York: Ballantine Books.

Hoopes, M., & Harper, J. (1987). *Birth order roles & sibling patterns in individual & family therapy.* Rockville, NY: Aspen Publishers.

Hough, A. (1991). *Let's have it out: The bare-bones manual of fair fighting.* Minneapolis, MN: Compcare Publishers.

James, M., & Savary L. (1977). *A new self: Self therapy with T.A.* Reading, MA: Addison-Wesley Publishing.

Kaufman, G. (1989). *The psychology of shame.* New York: Springer Publishing.

Kellogg, T., & Harrison, M. (1990). *Broken toys, broken dreams.* Amherst, MA: BRAT Publishing.

Kennedy, W. (1971). *Child psychology.* Englewood Cliffs, NJ: Prentice-Hall.

Kritsberg, W. (1987). *Chronic shock.* Deerfield Beach, FL: Health Communications.

Laird, C. (1990). *Webster's new world thesaurus.* New York: Warner Books.

Lankton, C., & Lankton, S. (1989). *Tales of enchantment.* New York: Brunner/Mazel.

Lerner, H.G. (1985). *The dance of anger.* New York: Harper & Row.

Lewis, M. (1992). *Shame: The exposed self.* New York: The Free Press.

Maccoby, E.E. (1980). *Social development: Psychological growth and the parent-child relationships.* New York: Harcourt Brace Jovanovich.

Mason, M. (1990). *Facing the space between: Shame, the invisible dragon.* Speech at ACDF Conference; Sante Fe, New Mexico.

Masterson, J.F., & Klein, R. (Eds.). (1989). *Psychotherapy of the disorders of the self: The Masterson approach.* New York: Brunner/Mazel.

McFarland, B., & Baker-Baumann, T. (1990). *Shame and body image.* Deerfield Beach, FL: Health Communications.

McGoldrick, M., & Gerson, R. (1985). *Genograms in family assessment.* New York: W.W. Norton.

The Meadows. (1989). *Survivors' week.* Workshop presented in Wickenburg, Arizona.

Meara, M., Stone, J., Kelly, M., & Davis, R. (1985). *Growing up catholic.* New York: Doubleday.

Missildine, W.H. (1963). *Your inner child of the past.* New York: Simon & Schuster.

Napier, N.J. (1990). *Recreating your self: Help for adult children of dysfunctional families.* New York: W.W. Norton.

Norcross, J.C. (Ed.). (1986). *Handbook of eclectic psychotherapy.* New York: Brunner/Mazel.

Pollard, J.K. (1987). *Self parenting: The complete guide to your inner conversations.* Malibu, CA: Generic Human Studies Publishing.

Prochaska, J., & DiClemente, C. (1986). The transtheoretical approach. In J. Norcross (Ed.), *Handbook of eclectic psychotherapy* (pp. 163-200). New York: Brunner/Mezel.

Prochaska, J., DiClemente, C., & Norcross, J. (1992). In search of how people change: Applications to Addictive Behaviors. *American Psychologist,* 47(9), 1102-1114.

Small, J. (1982). *Transformers.* Marina del Rey, CA: DeVorss & Company, Publisher.

Steiner, C. (1974). *Scripts people live.* New York: Grove Press.

Subby, R. (1990). *Healing the family within.* Speech at ACDF Convention, Sante Fe, New Mexico.

Tatem, D. (1989). *Codependency.* A lecture given at Lutheran Medical Center, Omaha, Nebraska.

Walen, S., DiGuiseppe, R., & Wessler, R. (1980). *A practitioner's guide to rational-emotive therapy.* New York: Oxford University Press.

Walter, D.L. (1989). *Forgiving our parents.* Minneapolis, MN: Compcare Publishers.

Weinrib, E.L. (1983). *Images of the self: The sand play therapy process.* Boston, MA: Sigo Press.

Wheeler, G. (1991). *Gestault reconsidered: A new approach to contact and resistance.* New York: Gardner Press.

Whitfield, C. (1987). *Healing the child within.* Deerfield Beach, FL: Health Communications.

Woititz J., & Garner, A. (1990). *Life skills for adult children.* Deerfield Beach, FL: Health Communications.

Woititz, J., & Garner, A. (1991). *Workbook: Life skills for adult children.* Deerfield Beach, FL: Health Communications.

Wolf, E.S. (1988). *Treating the self: Elements of clinical self psychology.* New York: The Guilford Press.

INDEX

cognitive 9, 11
expressive 38, 39
Gestalt 2, 11
inner child 5-26
levels of 20
massage 38
overview 5-26
rational-emotive 9
psychoanalytic 8
stage of change 7
strategic 8
timing 10
transtheoretical
Therapist
as educator 20
inner child issues 20
reaction as cues 46-7
Timing
therapy 10

Transactional Analysis 2, 9, 10-1
Trauma 39
Treatment
sessions 18
Treatment modality
group versus individual 17-8

V

Velcro kids 46-7
Veterans Administration Medical
Center (VAMC) 1
Visualization 33-4

W

Weinrib, E.L. 39, 63
Woititz, J. 53, 63
Wounded child 14

ABOUT
THE
AUTHOR

Ann E. Potter

Anne E. Potter, a licensed, certified psychologist and a registered nurse, has expertise in working with and speaking about addiction, codependency, and adult children of dysfunctional families; particularly trauma resolution and body image in eating disorders. Dr. Potter is active with a colleague in a program of research developing the *Children's Roles Inventory*, an assessment tool for therapists' use with children and adult children from alcoholic families. She has had articles published in *Lifestyles* and the *Journal of Studies on Alcohol* and article in press with *Education and Psychological Measurement.*

Dr. Potter earned a bachelor's degree in Nursing from Creighton University, an M.S. degree in Agency Counseling from the University of Nebraska at Omaha, and a doctorate in Counseling Psychology from the University of Nebraska at Lincoln. Her careers as a nurse, educator, therapist, and psychologist have provided her with almost twenty years of experience in the mental health and addiction fields.

Currently, Dr. Potter co-owns Therapy Resource Associates, Inc., a unique private practice in Omaha, Nebraska, that incorporates health and wellness concepts with the more traditional mental health therapies. She is the director of The Safe Place Programs for trauma resolution in which she practices Inner Child Therapy with clients and through which she trains professionals in Inner Child Therapy.

For information about Inner Child Therapy treatment programs and therapist training programs, please contact

Ann E. Potter, Ph.D.
Therapy Resource Associates
10855 W. Dodge Road, Suite 180
Omaha, NE 68154
(402)-330-6060